LONGMAN ORIGINALS Stage Fou
Series editor: Robert O'Neill

CW00402874

INSPECTOR THACKERAY *investigates*

Kenneth James and
Lloyd Mullen

Illustrations by Mark Oldroyd

 LONGMAN

Contents

An inside job

VERNON LANE

Scene 1

(Manchester Central Police Station. The office of Inspector Thackeray and Sergeant Silver. The phone rings.)

THACKERAY *(Lifts the phone)* Manchester Central Police Station. Detective Inspector Thackeray speaking. Yes… Is he hurt badly?… Fifty thousand pounds, you say… Park Street Hospital. Yes I've got that… Yes. I'll be there in about ten minutes. *(He puts the phone down.)* Sergeant!

SILVER Yes, sir.

THACKERAY I need a road map of the city centre.

SILVER But you've already got one, sir.

THACKERAY I had one. It was under the leg of this table.

SILVER Under the leg of the table, sir!

THACKERAY Yes, one leg's shorter than the other three. I suppose the cleaner's moved it. I can't think where

SILVER It's not under those papers on your desk, is it, sir?

THACKERAY If it is, I can't see it. Tell me, Silver, how do you keep your desk top empty?

SILVER No problem, sir. I put things away when I've finished with them.

THACKERAY Oh! Do you? Well you can tell me where your map is, then.

SILVER In this file. Under M for Manchester. Here we are, sir. What did you want to find?

THACKERAY Vernon Lane.

SILVER Oh, I know Vernon Lane without a map. If you go from here along London Road, and then turn right past the Palace cinema –

THACKERAY Yes?

SILVER Well, that's Vernon Lane.

THACKERAY Ah yes, of course. Vernon Lane. It's that little old narrow street between the new offices. It used to be called Empire Street.

SILVER Yes, they re-named it last year. It leads into Oxford Road.

THACKERAY That's very good, Silver. You've learned a lot in your time here.

SILVER I take the map home with me every night and learn it, sir. I have also learned the times of the trains to London and the international flights from Manchester airport.

THACKERAY Have you?

SILVER Yes, sir. They told us to do that at the police college. A good detective should –

THACKERAY All right, lad. All right. You've given me three lessons from that police college of yours already this week. Now put your coat on. We're going out.

SILVER Vernon Lane, sir?

THACKERAY No. Not Vernon Lane. You can take me to Park Street Hospital first. We'll use your car. I'm sure the police college taught you how to drive...

Scene 2

(In the police car. Sergeant Silver is driving.)

THACKERAY Do you always drive so carefully?

SILVER On duty? Yes, sir.

THACKERAY I want to get there today, you know.

SILVER Why are we going to the hospital?

THACKERAY There's been a robbery. A courier was hit on the head.

SILVER   What was he carrying? Money, I suppose?

THACKERAY   Yes. He was carrying more than fifty thousand pounds. Come on, lad. You can go faster than this. We've got work to do.

SILVER   Well sir, our speed on this road shouldn't be more than –

THACKERAY   Silver, if you give me one more lesson, you'll get out and walk.

SILVER   Sorry, sir. *(Pause)* Oh – Vernon Lane ahead, sir. On the right. Is that where it happened?

THACKERAY   Yes. Slow down here, slow down. Stop at this corner.

SILVER   You mean – park? Right at the corner? But you shouldn't –

THACKERAY   *(With a small cough)* Do you want to tell me something, lad?

SILVER   No, sir.

(The car slowly comes to a stop.)

THACKERAY   Right. Hm. It's not really a street at all. Cars are only allowed to drive as far as that underground car park on the right.

SILVER   Really? They didn't show that on the map.

THACKERAY   Ah. Well, that's something you don't know.

SILVER   So the courier was walking.

THACKERAY   Yes. But he didn't get very far. Just past the car park, in fact.

SILVER   What time was that?

THACKERAY   Ten past nine.

SILVER   It must have been very quiet at that time of day.

THACKERAY Yes. The thief chose a good time.

SILVER And a good place.

THACKERAY All right, Sergeant. Let's move on. I want to get to that hospital.

SILVER Right. *(He starts the car and they move off.)* Was there only one thief?

THACKERAY Well, we don't know till we ask the courier.

SILVER He can talk, then?

THACKERAY He couldn't talk much ten minutes ago, when the doctor phoned. But he should be able to now.

SILVER What happened to him?

THACKERAY The doctor said he was hit on the back of the head. It nearly knocked him out.

SILVER Was he one of our men?

THACKERAY Do you mean an ex-policeman?

SILVER Yes. A lot of ex-policemen work for security firms, you know.

THACKERAY Is that a fact?

SILVER Yes – oh. Sorry, sir. I suppose you knew that already.

THACKERAY This man was in the army before he became a courier.

SILVER Which security firm does he work for?

THACKERAY Safemen.

SILVER Safemen Security Limited. I've got a file on them.

THACKERAY I should have known.

SILVER They started about ten years ago. A small company. That's all I can remember, though.

THACKERAY You surprise me. They have about twenty-five people working for them, I believe. They're supposed to be quite good.

SILVER Who found the courier?

THACKERAY A woman. She phoned us.

SILVER *(Pause)* Here's the hospital now, sir.

THACKERAY Good. Park round the side.

SILVER Do they know we're coming?

THACKERAY Yes. They're expecting us. We can go straight in.

SILVER Which ward is he in? Do you know?

THACKERAY Ward Three. In a private room, at the end.

SILVER Do we know his name?

THACKERAY Roberts. Michael Roberts.

(Sergeant Silver parks the car. The two men get out and walk into the hospital.)

Scene 3

(Park Street Hospital. Ward Three. Mr Roberts is in bed. The two policemen are standing beside him.)

SILVER Mr Roberts? Mr Roberts?

THACKERAY The medicine's made him sleepy. Mr Roberts – can you hear me?

ROBERTS Uh. Yes. A drink. Can I have a drink?

THACKERAY The water's beside you, Silver.

SILVER Right.

ROBERTS Who are you?

THACKERAY I'm a police officer.

ROBERTS Yes, yes. Police.

SILVER Here you are. Drink this. I'll hold the glass. No, don't sit up. That's it.

ROBERTS Thank you. Thank you.

THACKERAY What happened, Mr Roberts?

ROBERTS He hit me. On the head.

THACKERAY Who hit you?

ROBERTS A man. Hit me. And then there was a woman. I saw a woman. My briefcase. Where's my briefcase? Where's it gone?

THACKERAY Forget the briefcase. Who hit you?

ROBERTS He came from behind me. From my right. Hit me on the head. Where's my briefcase?

THACKERAY Who? Who hit you? Could you see him?

ROBERTS No. I didn't see him.

SILVER Did you see anything?

ROBERTS Shoes. Yes – shoes. Black shoes. Very clean. Ooh! My head!

THACKERAY We'd better leave him, Sergeant.

SILVER Yes. He's going to sleep again.

THACKERAY A man. And black shoes.

SILVER And a woman? Who was she, d'you think, sir?

THACKERAY Perhaps it was the woman who phoned the police.

SILVER Or perhaps she was with the man.

THACKERAY Possible. Come on. Let him sleep.

(They walk out of the room, towards the hospital entrance.)

SILVER What do you think, sir?

THACKERAY Probably an inside job.

SILVER An inside job?

THACKERAY Yes. The thief was either someone who worked at this security firm. Or someone who worked at the bank.

SILVER The courier was carrying the money to the bank, I suppose.

THACKERAY Yes. Or even someone who worked in Travel Tours itself.

SILVER Travel Tours – that's the firm that lost the money, is it?

THACKERAY Yes. A lot of these robberies are inside jobs.

SILVER Which of the three is the most likely, d'you think?

THACKERAY I'll tell you after I've talked to them all.

(The two policemen have reached the hospital entrance. They go outside.)

SILVER Where do we go first?

THACKERAY Safemen Security. You can take us there now. *(They get into the car.)* You won't drive too fast, will you?

SILVER On duty? Oh no sir. I always –

THACKERAY It was a joke, Sergeant, a joke.

SILVER Oh. Sorry, sir.

THACKERAY Don't apologise, lad. Just try to laugh next time, eh? Now let's see what Mr Lock has to say.

SILVER Mr Lock?

THACKERAY He's in charge of Safemen Security. He's the one to see first.

MESSAGE

TIME: 9.40

SENDER: Sgt. Smith

DETAILS: Michael Roberts (Safemen courier) taking money from Travel Tours to bank
– hit on head, robbed (£50,000 plus)
– in Vernon Lane, just past car park
– woman telephoned police
– now in Park Street Hospital, Ward 3

Park Street Hospital 10.00 am

Roberts (R) – couldn't talk v. well but clear about this:

1. Man came from behind, right.
2. Hit R on head.
3. R saw black shoes
4. R saw woman later (with man? or phoned police?)

R worried about briefcase – must talk to him later.
Inside job? Possibly Safemen itself/ Bank/Travel Tours.
Who knew what was inside briefcase?

Scene 4

(Safemen Security Limited. The manager's office.)

LOCK It's very bad for our name, I'm afraid. Very bad for our name. But we can't help that now.

SILVER Has it ever happened before, Mr Lock?

LOCK No. We've been in business for ten years. And this is the first time.

THACKERAY What do you know about the attack, sir?

LOCK Nothing. Well – the police told me very little when they rang.

THACKERAY Well, tell us about your courier, Roberts. How old is he?

LOCK Fifty-seven last July.

SILVER Fifty-seven!

LOCK True. He is rather old for courier work. He usually works in the office these days.

THACKERAY Why didn't he stay there this morning?

LOCK A lot of our people are ill this week. So I had to ask Roberts to do the Travel Tours job. He's fit and healthy, and he's worked as a courier before. Besides, it's a very short distance from Travel Tours to the bank.

SILVER That's true, sir. They're both on Vernon Lane.

THACKERAY You chose Roberts yourself, did you?

LOCK Yes. A mistake, I suppose.

THACKERAY Mm. Who usually carries the Travel Tours money?

LOCK There's no special man. In fact two men usually do it together. For larger amounts, we like to use two men in uniform.

SILVER Was Roberts in uniform, sir?

LOCK No, he was in his own clothes.

THACKERAY   And he did the job alone.

LOCK   Yes. I told you. We had no one else to send. Nine of our men are ill.

SILVER   What did Roberts carry the money in, Mr Lock?

LOCK   A briefcase. A black briefcase.

THACKERAY   It's Wednesday today. Do Travel Tours always bank their money on Wednesdays?

LOCK   No, they choose a different day every week.

SILVER   Exactly how much money was Roberts carrying?

LOCK   Fifty thousand and thirty pounds.

SILVER   As much as that?

LOCK   I'm afraid so. Yes.

SILVER   What time did he leave their building?

LOCK   Well – Roberts reached Travel Tours at exactly eight-thirty. The assistant phoned us to check that he was one of our men.

THACKERAY   That's usual, is it?

LOCK   Yes, it is. Then they counted the money together. Roberts left their building at exactly five past nine.

THACKERAY   Are you getting all this, Silver?

SILVER   Yes, sir, I'm writing it all down.

LOCK   The assistant walked to the door with him, and saw him turn into Vernon Lane. The bank is at the other end, only a hundred metres away.

SILVER   Just a minute, sir – if it's so near, why don't Travel Tours carry the money themselves?

LOCK   The money must be carried by a security company. If it isn't, the insurance companies won't insure it.

THACKERAY   I see. What happened next?

13

SAFEMEN SECURITY
- in business for ten years
- small firm (25 people)
- have a 'good name' – this is their first trouble

LOCK – safemen manager
- heard about robbery from us
- ex-policeman, knows his job
- usually sends two men in uniform for large amounts
- 9 people ill (?? check this!) so asked Roberts to do
  Travel Tours job
- in his office at time of robbery
Lock is sure no one from safemen stole the money.

LOCK ON ROBERTS
1. Age 57, fit and healthy, worked as courier before.
2. Now works in office.
3. Was carrying £50,030.

LOCK ON TIMES etc
1. Roberts reached Travel Tours about 8.30.
2. TT assistant phoned safemen to check.
3. Roberts and assistant counted money.
4. Left building at 9.05.

LOCK A phone call from Manchester Central Police Station. They said a woman had found Roberts in Vernon Lane. He'd been knocked out.

THACKERAY Mr Lock – could anyone in your company have helped the thief?

LOCK No. *(Pause)* Look, Inspector, I was fifteen years in the police myself before this job. I know an honest man when I see one. And I've chosen all these men myself. So I think I can say no.

THACKERAY Have you any idea who could have done it?

LOCK No idea at all. Perhaps it is an inside job. But it won't be anyone from here.

THACKERAY Mm. Before we go, could we have a photograph of Roberts?

LOCK Yes, here you are. We keep photographs of all our couriers.

THACKERAY It may help us later on. *(Pause)* Well, that's all for the moment, sir.

LOCK I won't come to the door with you, Inspector. I have so much work to do.

SILVER Inspector – may I say something?

THACKERAY Of course.

SILVER Mr Lock, one of your men was badly hurt. You've lost a lot of money. You don't seem to be very surprised.

LOCK Just think for a moment, Sergeant. If there were no thieves, there'd be no security firms. There are a lot of people who want to steal money. And my men carry a lot of money. Why should I be surprised? I don't like it, but I'm not going to cry about it. It's a hard life. But I knew that when I started this business. Any other questions, Sergeant?

15

SILVER No sir.

THACKERAY We'll be on our way then. Thank you, Mr Lock.
You've been most helpful.

Scene 5

(In the car. Sergeant Silver is driving.)

SILVER If I turn right at the corner, it will take us to
Vernon Lane. We *are* going to Travel Tours, aren't
we?

THACKERAY That's right. As quick as you like.

SILVER He's a hard man, Lock.

THACKERAY But a good one.

SILVER He only sent *one* courier.

THACKERAY He's a real old-time policeman. He's honest. He
stands up straight. He has his hair cut every
Saturday. And he knows his job.

SILVER Yes, but don't you think he's *too* old-time, sir?
The job has changed a lot since he began.

THACKERAY That reminds me, Silver. You ought to get your
hair cut this Saturday. It's a bit long at the back,
don't you think?

SILVER I'm so busy, sir, and I can never remember things
like that, sir.

THACKERAY Open a file, then, open a file. Under H for
haircut.

SILVER Sir. Ah, here we are – Travel Tours. Who are we
seeing?

THACKERAY A Mr Rich. He owns the place. He's expecting us.
You'd better lock the car; we don't want another
robbery...

Scene 6

(Travel Tours Limited. The owner's office. Mr Rich is at his desk. The door opens. The two policemen enter.)

RICH Come in, gentlemen, come in. My name is Rich. I'm glad to see you. What a terrible day. Terrible. Please sit down.

THACKERAY *(Closes the door)* Thank you. *(Pause)* Any more news of the robbery, Mr Rich?

RICH News? Here? None at all. I thought you might have some.

THACKERAY Well, the courier's in hospital.

RICH Poor old chap. I'm sorry for him. Really sorry. But Safemen are to blame.

SILVER Why are they to blame, sir?

RICH Well, you need young men for this kind of job, don't you? He must have been well over fifty. I mean – sending a man like that. Really!

THACKERAY Would you mind answering a few questions, Mr Rich?

RICH Not at all. Not at all. Go right ahead.

THACKERAY Are you insured against robbery?

RICH Insured? Of course I'm insured. But I need the money now. Insurance companies take such a long time to pay, you know.

SILVER Why don't your customers pay by cheque or bank card?

RICH If they pay by cash and make a reservation early, they get the holiday cheaper. We don't have to pay bank charges. We sell more holidays. So we make more money. It's good business. *(Laughs)* It *was* good business until this happened. This will finish me, you know.

THACKERAY It will, if you don't help us, Mr Rich. Just answer my questions. Now – was the robbery planned, d'you think?

RICH But how could it be? We send the money at a different time every week.

THACKERAY So you think it happened by chance?

RICH Probably someone was just walking down Vernon Lane – he saw the briefcase and he thought he'd steal it.

SILVER And then found fifty thousand pounds in it? Quite a nice surprise!

THACKERAY And not very likely!

RICH It's very quiet in that street, at that time of morning. Anybody could have come up behind the courier. Anybody. They could easily have hit him on the head, then run off with the briefcase.

THACKERAY Anything is *possible*, I suppose. But now, can we go back to the beginning?

RICH Well, yesterday afternoon, I asked Mr Pound to bank the week's money in the usual way.

SILVER Mr Pound?

RICH My assistant. He helps me to run the office here.

THACKERAY I'll see him later. Make a note of the name, Sergeant.

RICH You can talk to him now if you like, Inspector. He really knows more about it than me. In fact, he gave the money to the courier. I never even saw the man.

THACKERAY You never even saw him?

RICH No. My office here is very quiet. I never see anybody except visitors, like you.

THACKERAY All right. You asked Pound to bank the money. What then?

RICH He phoned Safemen.

THACKERAY Did anybody else know about the money?

RICH Yes, of course. The whole office knew.

SILVER The whole office!

RICH Yes. When I say the whole office – I just mean the three people on this floor. Of course, the four who work in the travel shop downstairs – they don't know anything about the money.

THACKERAY Mm. What did Pound do then?

RICH He fixed everything as usual, I suppose.

THACKERAY So Safemen sent their man here this morning?

RICH Yes, but he never got to the bank.

THACKERAY No, he didn't. *(Pause)* Now the Safemen courier was carrying a briefcase. An ordinary briefcase. So why would anyone take it, d'you think?

RICH Well, I don't know, do I? But things like this do happen. You read it in the papers every day. A black briefcase like that always looks as if it might have lots of money inside. Don't you think so?

THACKERAY Possibly.

SILVER What time did you get to the office this morning, Mr Rich?

RICH About twenty to nine, I think. Twenty to nine. Yes, about then.

THACKERAY Good. Thank you Mr Rich. Don't worry. We'll do our best to get your money back.

RICH Oh, it's too late for that. Far too late. We'll never get the money back. This is a bad day for Travel Tours. A terrible, terrible day.

THACKERAY Could we see your assistant now, please? Mr Pound?

RICH But of course. I'll take you to his office.

SILVER Don't worry sir. We'll find our own way. We passed it when we came in.

Scene 7

(The assistant's office. Mr Pound is at his desk.)

THACKERAY Mr Pound. My name's Thackeray and this is Sergeant Silver.

POUND Ah yes. You've come about the robbery of course.

THACKERAY Yes. We just want to ask you about a few things, Mr Pound.

POUND Yes, certainly, Inspector.

THACKERAY When did you first hear about it?

POUND The robbery? About nine-thirty. Safemen phoned us with the news.

SILVER What time had Roberts left here, sir?

POUND It must have been about ten past nine.

THACKERAY So it was twenty minutes before you heard of the robbery?

POUND Yes.

THACKERAY Had you ever met Roberts before?

POUND Never. I asked for his Safemen courier's card, and then I checked the number with them by phone.

SILVER Is that what you usually do?

POUND Yes, it's the usual check. It's always worked before.

THACKERAY And that's all you know about him? His number?

POUND Yes. That's all we ever know about our couriers.

SILVER Was this money in bags, Mr Pound?

POUND Yes, in bags. Just like these on my desk.

THACKERAY All right. Thank you. May I see the other people in the office?

POUND Well there's only Miss Matthews, the secretary.

THACKERAY All right. Could we see her?

POUND Yes, of course, Inspector. *(He picks up the telephone on his desk.)* Miss Matthews! Would you come in for a moment, please. *(He puts the telephone down.)*

THACKERAY We'll have to talk to her alone, Mr Pound.

POUND Oh yes, of course. You can use this office. *(The door opens. Miss Matthews enters.)*

MATTHEWS Mr Pound?

POUND Oh, come in, Miss Matthews. These two gentlemen would like to ask you some questions.

MATTHEWS Me?

POUND Yes. They won't keep you long. I'll be back in a few minutes. *(He goes out.)*

THACKERAY Sit down Miss Matthews. Now then, you are the office secretary?

MATTHEWS Yes, that's right.

THACKERAY Well, I'm Inspector Thackeray. And this is Sergeant Silver. We're from the police.

MATTHEWS You're wasting your time with me, Inspector. I know nothing.

THACKERAY When did you join this firm?

MATTHEWS Travel Tours? In February this year.

THACKERAY And where were you before?

MATTHEWS In Croydon. With a supermarket.

SILVER What did you do there, Miss Matthews?

MATTHEWS The same as I do here.

SILVER And what's that?

MATTHEWS As little as possible. I'm a secretary. D'you know what that means? I write down other people's words all day. I send them to people I don't know. When they write back, do I get a chance to reply? Oh no. Somebody else replies. I write it down and send it. I'm a machine. So don't ask me to say I love my work. Because I don't. And don't expect me to cry about a few thousand pounds. I'll care about this office when this office cares about me.

THACKERAY Forgive me for asking, Miss Matthews. But have you ever been in trouble with the police?

MATTHEWS Certainly not.

THACKERAY How much do you know about today's robbery?

MATTHEWS Nothing at all.

SILVER When did you get here, Miss Matthews?

MATTHEWS About ten past nine.

SILVER Doesn't your work start at nine o'clock?

MATTHEWS It starts when I get here.

THACKERAY So when you arrived, the courier had gone?

MATTHEWS Yes.

THACKERAY So you never saw him?

MATTHEWS No. I told you – you're wasting your time. I know nothing.

SILVER Who knew about the money Miss Matthews?

MATTHEWS Mr Pound and Mr Rich. And me.

THACKERAY Who did it, d'you think?

MATTHEWS Mm, you're the policeman. You tell me.

THACKERAY One last thing, Miss Matthews. I want you to look at this photograph. *(He shows her the photograph.)*

MATTHEWS Who's he?

THACKERAY Haven't you ever seen him before? Anywhere?

MATTHEWS No. Is he the courier they've all been talking about? *(She returns the photograph.)*

THACKERAY That will be all, Miss Matthews.

MATTHEWS A pleasure, I'm sure. Can I go now?

THACKERAY For the moment. Stay in the building, won't you? We may want to speak to you again.

MATTHEWS I'm not going anywhere. I have got a job, you know.

THACKERAY Good morning, Miss Matthews.

(Miss Matthews goes out.)

SILVER Well sir? That's all of them.

THACKERAY Yes.

SILVER And every one of them is wearing black shoes.

THACKERAY Yes. Even Miss Matthews.

SILVER But there is one more I'd like to see, sir.

THACKERAY Oh?

SILVER The man at the main door. The porter.

THACKERAY Hmm.

SILVER You don't seem very interested.

TRAVEL TOURS (TT)
- small travel/holiday firm
- 3 people working in office/ 4 in shop downstairs
- Mr Rich, owner (early 40s?) expensive clothes, nice office

RICH

1. Blames safemen, says courier was too old.
2. Sends TT money at <u>different</u> times each week, so robbery difficult to plan.
3. Everyone in TT office knew about money, Pound arranged courier yesterday.
4. Never saw courier, says he was in his office all the time.
5. Thinks someone just saw black briefcase – worth a lot, so stole it. Chance?

POUND

(Age: mid 20s, big, quiet, helpful)
- asked Roberts for card, made phone check
- counted money into bags
- says Roberts left at 9.10

MISS MATTHEWS

(Age: about 22 – argues a lot, not v. helpful)
- says her last job was in Croydon supermarket
- hates her work
- arrived 9.10 (late!)
- never saw courier, but knew about money
- never in trouble with the police (check this)
- does not recognise photo of courier

THACKERAY Well, yes I am. But I want another word with Mr Pound first.

SILVER While you're doing that perhaps I can talk to the porter, then.

THACKERAY Yes. All right.

SILVER And may I take this photograph of Roberts with me?

THACKERAY Yes. And tell Mr Pound on your way out that I'd like to see him. There's something I forgot to ask him before. Something that could be important to us, I think.

Scene 8

(Travel Tours entrance hall. The porter's desk.)

SILVER Excuse me a minute, please. Could I have a few words with you?

PORTER What about?

SILVER You're the porter here?

PORTER Who wants to know?

SILVER I do. Sergeant Silver. Police.

PORTER A police sergeant! With long hair like that? You're a bit young, aren't you?

SILVER Just answer the questions, please.

PORTER You haven't asked any yet. Where's that inspector?

SILVER Upstairs.

PORTER Talking to somebody important, I suppose.

SILVER Have you been at this desk all morning?

PORTER That's what they pay me for.

SILVER Have you or haven't you?

PORTER Of course I have. I work a full day here. I start at eight, and finish at four. Not like some people.

SILVER I want you to look at this photograph.

PORTER Who is it?

SILVER You tell me.

PORTER Oh yes. I know him.

SILVER Well?

PORTER It's that courier, isn't it?

SILVER When did you last see him?

PORTER This morning.

SILVER When?

PORTER He came in here when I was giving Mr Rich the morning's letters.

SILVER Did you talk to him?

PORTER Did I talk to him! With telephones, with people coming in, and going out – when have I got time to talk to people?

SILVER What did you do then?

PORTER I asked for his card. I wasn't sure about him.

SILVER Why not?

PORTER He didn't look like a Safemen courier, did he? He wasn't wearing a uniform. And he was alone – there should have been two of them.

SILVER So what did you do?

PORTER I sent him up to Mr Pound's office.

SILVER Was Mr Rich still with you when the courier came down again?

PORTER No. Mr Rich had gone back to his car for something. I was alone then.

SILVER And which way did the courier go out of here?

PORTER He went out through the front door, of course. What d'you think?

SILVER So he went through the main door, into London Road, round the corner, and down Vernon Lane towards the bank.

PORTER Don't ask me. I stay inside here. I don't know where they go.

SILVER When did Miss Matthews come in?

PORTER Ah. I do know that. She came in just after the courier had walked out.

SILVER Did she, indeed! *(Pause)* Tell me. Where's the car park?

PORTER You're standing on it.

SILVER Don't be funny. Unless you want to answer these questions in the police station.

PORTER It's the truth, Sergeant. It's under this floor. Below ground.

SILVER How do people get there? And don't tell me they drive in. I mean from here.

PORTER Through that door behind me at the back. And before you ask me about the cars – they get in from London Road. They turn into Vernon Lane. The entrance to the car park's on the right.

SILVER So Mr Rich went through that door at the back to his car.

PORTER That's right.

SILVER And how long were you away from this desk?

27

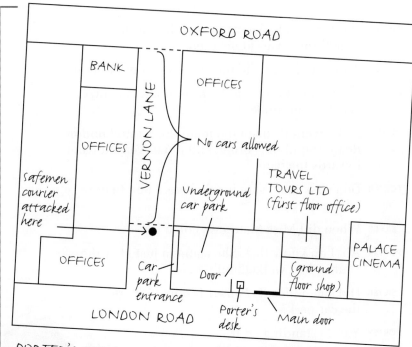

OXFORD ROAD

BANK

OFFICES

VERNON LANE

OFFICES

No cars allowed

safemen
courier
attacked
here

Underground
car park

TRAVEL
TOURS LTD
(first floor office)

OFFICES

Car
park
entrance

Door

(ground
floor shop)

PALACE
CINEMA

LONDON ROAD

Porter's
desk

Main door

PORTER'S STORY

(from Sgt. Silver)

– argued a lot, not v. helpful

1. Courier arrived when he was giving letters to Rich.
2. He checked courier – looked at his card.
3. He sent courier up to Pound's office.
4. He was alone when courier came down again. (Rich had gone to his car.)
5. Courier left through the main door.
6. He never left his desk.
7. Miss Matthews arrived just after courier left the building.

PORTER Don't try to be clever, Sergeant. I never said I left it. In fact, I've been here since I got in this morning.

SILVER I'll have to check that, of course.

PORTER Now just a minute. What are you suggesting?

SILVER I'm not suggesting anything. Now, your name is...?

PORTER Dorman. With one 'o'.

SILVER Right then, Dorman.

PORTER They usually call me *Mr* Dorman.

SILVER I may need you again later.

PORTER Another little talk? That'll be nice. Glad to see you any time. Tell your friends. I'm always here, all day and every day.

Scene 9

(Mr Pound's office. The Inspector is questioning Mr Pound.)

THACKERAY I'm sorry to take so much of your time, Mr Pound. But I was wondering about something else.

POUND Yes?

THACKERAY Why didn't you go with the courier to the bank?

POUND Me? It's not my job.

THACKERAY No, but this morning was different, surely?

POUND How d'you mean, different?

THACKERAY Well, Safemen usually send two men in uniform. Today they only sent one – Roberts, in ordinary clothes.

POUND I'm not paid to do that sort of thing, Inspector. It could be dangerous.

THACKERAY Yes. We've discovered that. But he'd have been glad of help. He was over fifty, wasn't he? And you're a fairly big man.

POUND Over fifty? Was he really? D'you know, I never noticed. Over fifty, eh?

THACKERAY Didn't you see him very well, Mr Pound? You gave him the money.

POUND Yes, I know. But I was watching the money, not his face.

THACKERAY What was he wearing?

POUND Coat and hat, I think. Yes, I remember saying goodbye to him at the door downstairs. He was wearing a coat and hat.

THACKERAY Very good then, Mr Pound. That's all, thank you.

POUND Do you know who did it yet, Inspector?

THACKERAY I think so.

POUND When can you tell us?

THACKERAY That depends on Mr Roberts. If he gets better quickly I might be able to tell you this afternoon.

Scene 10

Inspector Thackeray explains

(Travel Tours Limited. Mr Rich's office.)

THACKERAY Well, Mr Rich. We've come back to your office this afternoon because I've got one or two more questions.

RICH More questions? But what about the thief? And the money? That's what I want to know.

SILVER You will, Mr Rich. In a minute or two.

(The door opens. Miss Matthews comes in.)

MATTHEWS Excuse me, Mr Rich. You asked to see me?

THACKERAY No, Miss Matthews. *I* asked.

MATTHEWS *(Closing the door)* Me? Why me? I don't know anything. I told you that.

SILVER We checked everything you told us.

MATTHEWS It's all true. Everything I've told you is true.

SILVER Quite right. You worked in a supermarket before this job.

MATTHEWS That's what I said.

SILVER But there's one thing you didn't tell us. You left after a robbery there.

MATTHEWS No, I didn't tell you that.

RICH Why not, Miss Matthews? I should have known that, too.

MATTHEWS Well, the robbery wasn't my fault. I didn't steal anything, did I?

THACKERAY Why did you leave immediately afterwards?

MATTHEWS I had to. Every time a company loses money, they get rid of people. The last person to join is the first one to leave.

SILVER Are you sure that's the reason?

MATTHEWS Of course I am. Check it if you like.

(Mr Roberts, the Safemen courier comes in. He is much better.)

ROBERTS Excuse me. Is this the right office?

RICH Good heavens! Are you better already? I thought you were in hospital.

THACKERAY Do you know Mr Roberts, sir?

RICH Well – no.

THACKERAY Then why are you so surprised that he is here? And how do you know he has been in hospital?

RICH But you're the courier, aren't you?

ROBERTS Yes sir.

SILVER But how did you know that?

RICH Well – I mean – I just guessed.

THACKERAY You just guessed? You can't guess a thing like that, sir. You either know him or you don't.

RICH Well, I suppose I know him then.

THACKERAY In that case, you must have seen him before.

RICH Perhaps I have. I can't think when.

ROBERTS I was at the porter's desk this morning, sir. You were looking at your letters.

RICH Ah yes. You were asking for Mr Pound.

ROBERTS That's right.

SILVER You didn't tell us that this morning, Mr Rich.

RICH Well, I didn't think it was important.

THACKERAY You saw the courier – but you didn't think it was important.

RICH I didn't know he was the courier.

SILVER You did, otherwise you wouldn't have recognised him now.

THACKERAY And how did you know the courier was an old man?

RICH Did I say that?

THACKERAY Yes. This morning, when you spoke to us.

SILVER That's correct, sir. It's written here in my notebook. You said, "He must have been well over fifty."

RICH Ah yes. Someone told me this morning. Miss Matthews, I think. Yes, Miss Matthews.

MATTHEWS I never said such a thing. So you can stop telling lies.

RICH Miss Matthews, I must ask you to keep quiet. You must let me take care of this.

MATTHEWS Take care? You think you can take care of anybody? Look at this poor man. He was in a hospital bed this morning. Can't you see he's still weak? You haven't even offered him a chair.

RICH Oh. Well, we seem to be using all the chairs. Perhaps – er...

MATTHEWS "Perhaps Miss Matthews will go and find one." Mr Rich won't go and find one of course. That would be too much trouble. Come along, Mr Roberts. I'll take you into the next office, and find you a comfortable chair.

ROBERTS Thank you, miss. It's all right. A car is waiting outside to take me home. The Inspector only wanted me to call in here for a minute.

RICH And perhaps Miss Matthews –

MATTHEWS "Perhaps Miss Matthews will come back to this job tomorrow." But she won't. I'm finished here, Mr Rich. I've had enough of you and your job. Here, take my arm, Mr Roberts.

ROBERTS Thank you.

MATTHEWS Oh dear, you're still a bit weak, aren't you? I know. I'll get you a nice cup of tea. Come along.

(They leave.)

RICH Well! Sorry about that. She gets rather emotional sometimes. Don't believe everything she says. She'll be back tomorrow.

SILVER I think you're wrong, sir.

THACKERAY You've been wrong about a lot of things, Mr Rich. Simple, little things. The briefcase, for example.

RICH The briefcase!

THACKERAY How did you know the courier had a briefcase?

RICH Me? I didn't know that.

THACKERAY You even knew the colour. Your notebook, Sergeant.

SILVER Here's what you said this morning: "A black briefcase like that always looks as if it might have lots of money inside."

RICH Oh, well, I remember now. I saw the briefcase at the porter's desk this morning.

SILVER But how did you know it was the courier's? In your interview this morning, you even said, "I never even saw the man." Look. It's here in my notebook.

THACKERAY Mr Rich. Why don't you take Miss Matthews' advice?

RICH What's that?

THACKERAY Stop telling lies.

RICH But Inspector –

THACKERAY The fact is, you needed money.

SILVER We checked with your bank. You owe them quite a lot.

THACKERAY You were at the porter's desk when the courier came in.

RICH But I didn't know him.

THACKERAY You heard his conversation with the porter.

RICH I didn't hear a word. I was opening my letters.

THACKERAY And you saw him go up to Mr Pound's office.

RICH Did I?

THACKERAY You knew that later he would come down with the money. And you knew he'd go round the corner – into Vernon Lane. To the bank.

RICH This is nonsense. Complete nonsense.

SILVER You went to the door at the back of the building. And down to the car park.

RICH Yes, I did that, certainly. I'd left my briefcase in the car.

SILVER You waited inside the car park entrance in Vernon Lane.

RICH This is just not true!

THACKERAY Oh, Mr Rich. Come on now. It was so easy, wasn't it? The courier was alone. He wasn't a young man. And he was carrying fifty thousand pounds.

SILVER The street was empty. You waited, and stepped out as he passed. You hit him on the head. Then you stepped back into the car park with the briefcase.

RICH But why should I steal my own money?

THACKERAY The same old reason as everybody else, Mr Rich. For the insurance. You keep the fifty thousand pounds in the briefcase. And the insurance company gives you another fifty thousand.

SILVER For five minutes' work.

THACKERAY But now you'll spend five years, Mr Rich –

RICH Five years –

THACKERAY In prison. Regretting it.

Dangerous medicine

Scene 1

(The house of Alec Granger, a rich businessman. Inspector Thackeray, who has just rung the bell, is waiting at the door with Sergeant Silver.)

THACKERAY Well, it's a lovely house. From the outside, at least.

SILVER D'you think they heard the bell?

THACKERAY It's always the same in these big houses. It takes them half an hour to walk to the front door.

SILVER Ah. There's somebody coming now.

THACKERAY Good morning, madam.

MRS WILLIS You're the police?

THACKERAY Yes. I'm Inspector Thackeray, and this is Sergeant Silver.

MRS WILLIS Please come in.

THACKERAY We had a phone call from Dr Brown. Is he still here?

MRS WILLIS Oh yes. I'm the housekeeper, Mrs Willis. Dr Brown is still in the living-room, with the body. I'll take you to him now.

Scene 2

(They go into the living-room of the house.)

MRS WILLIS Dr Brown... the police are here.

DR BROWN Ah. Thackeray. I'm glad you could come.

THACKERAY How are you, Dr Brown? I haven't seen you since that Portland Flats murder.

DR BROWN Ah, yes. The rich businessman and the game of chess. I remember that well. But that was more than two years ago, wasn't it?

THACKERAY You didn't meet Sergeant Silver then, did you? He really solved that case, you know.

DR BROWN Sergeant.

SILVER Morning, sir.

DR BROWN I'm terribly sorry to drag you out so early. But I think it's a job for the police.

SILVER This gentleman in the chair?

MRS WILLIS Mr Alec Granger. He owns this house. Or he did.

THACKERAY How long has he been dead?

DR BROWN He must have died last night... oh... between nine o'clock and ten o'clock. I couldn't be more exact than that.

THACKERAY Who found him?

MRS WILLIS I did.

THACKERAY When was that?

MRS WILLIS At half past eight this morning – just before I phoned Dr Brown.

THACKERAY All right, Doctor. You examined Mr Granger, then you phoned me. You must have had a good reason.

DR BROWN Yes. I have. His capsules.

SILVER Mr Granger's medicine, sir?

DR BROWN Yes. Perhaps first I'd better explain exactly what they are.

THACKERAY Just a minute. Where are these capsules?

MRS WILLIS They're in the bathroom cupboard. They're always kept there.

THACKERAY Right. First of all I'd like to have a look at them.

MRS WILLIS I'll show you the way.

DR BROWN No need, Mrs Willis. I'll take the Inspector up.

THACKERAY Mrs Willis – why don't you talk to Sergeant Silver here? Tell him all about this morning.

MRS WILLIS Very well.

THACKERAY Right, Doctor. You lead the way. *(They both go out.)*

SILVER Now then, Mrs Willis. You came into the room at half past eight. Tell me exactly what happened.

MRS WILLIS Well, I came in the door. The room was still dark, of course. I walked across to the window, and opened the curtains. Then I turned round and saw Mr Granger – just sitting there.

SILVER Have you moved him at all?

MRS WILLIS No, I haven't. He was sitting there just like that. In his usual chair.

SILVER This book on the floor beside him – was this here too?

MRS WILLIS Yes. He must have dropped it. Poor Mr Granger. He must have been very ill. He always looked after his books so carefully. Many of them are quite valuable, you know.

SILVER Yes, and all these old paintings too – the tables and chairs here – they must have cost thousands.

MRS WILLIS I love this house and all these beautiful things in it. And Mr Granger was always so good to me. I feel all empty now that he has died.

SILVER How long have you worked here, Mrs Willis?

MRS WILLIS I've been his housekeeper for twenty years. Twenty wonderful years.

Scene 3

(Dr Brown and Inspector Thackeray are walking towards the bathroom.)

DR BROWN Oh yes, she's an excellent housekeeper. She did everything for him, you know.

THACKERAY So Mrs Willis gave him his medicine – his capsules?

DR BROWN Most of the time, yes. She used to be a nurse, you know.

THACKERAY Oh, did she? What was wrong with Granger?

DR BROWN Heart trouble.

THACKERAY Bad?

DR BROWN Very. He was in hospital with it last year.

THACKERAY But if his heart just failed, why did you phone us?

DR BROWN Ah, this is the bathroom. *(He opens the door.)* The capsules are in a bottle in that cupboard. I'll open it and you can have a look.

THACKERAY There are so many bottles here. Which one?

DR BROWN The one next to the syringe. On the bottom shelf.

THACKERAY Next to the syringe? Oh yes. I can see now. It's that big bottle, isn't it? I shan't touch it. There may be fingerprints on it.

DR BROWN You can see through the glass.

THACKERAY Yes. Three green capsules.

DR BROWN That's the trouble. There should be four.

THACKERAY Why's that?

DR BROWN It's like this. Every Monday morning, I give him a new bottle of capsules. I count them into the bottle. Seven. One capsule for every day of the week. Seven. Never more. Never less.

THACKERAY And today's Thursday.

DR BROWN Right. Monday, Tuesday, Wednesday – three gone. There should still be four in the bottle.

THACKERAY Suppose he takes an extra one – what then?

DR BROWN He dies in about fifteen minutes.

THACKERAY Did he know that?

DR BROWN Certainly. He had to know.

THACKERAY So if someone gave him two instead of one?

DR BROWN He'd never take them. He knew the danger.

THACKERAY So you want the police doctor to open him up?

DR BROWN Yes. I think your people should look inside the stomach. Then we'll know whether he really took two capsules.

THACKERAY Mrs Willis knew about these capsules. Did anyone else?

DR BROWN Two other people at least. His nephew and his niece. John and Ann Edwards.

THACKERAY Did they all know that an extra capsule would kill him?

DR BROWN Oh yes. Besides, it's written there on the bottle.

THACKERAY Could anyone buy extra capsules, d'you think?

DR BROWN Good heavens, no. You can't get these things in a shop. They usually only give them to people in hospital. They're the very latest thing. They're changing them all the time.

THACKERAY How d'you mean?

DR BROWN Well, look at those in the bottle for example. They're the green ones. They're new. Granger got them for the first time this week. They've got slightly less nitrine in them.

THACKERAY What did he have before?

DR BROWN Red ones. He's always had red ones. Until Monday.

THACKERAY They look soft, like green jelly.

DR BROWN Yes, they are soft. The medicine is inside.

THACKERAY What does it look like?

DR BROWN The medicine? Oh, a bit like water, I suppose. The capsule's about half full of it. The outside slowly breaks up in the stomach, and the medicine runs out.

THACKERAY So. One capsule keeps him alive. Two capsules kill him. Right?

DR BROWN That's it.

THACKERAY Well, if he did take two, we have quite a problem. How d'you persuade a man to take something that's going to kill him?

DR BROWN That's a question you'll have to answer, not me.

THACKERAY Perhaps it's time we asked Mrs Willis then. Or perhaps she's told my sergeant the answer already.

Scene 4

(The dining room. Sergeant Silver is questioning Mrs Willis.)

SILVER Now then, Mrs Willis. This table here. It's been set for three people. Last night's dinner, was it?

MRS WILLIS Yes. Mr Granger always had people to dinner on Wednesday night.

SILVER Who?

MRS WILLIS Usually his nephew – Mr John Edwards. And his niece – Miss Ann Edwards.

SILVER But only two of these meals were eaten. Nobody's touched this third plate. Who didn't come?

MRS WILLIS I'm afraid I don't know.

SILVER You don't know? But weren't you here last night?

MRS WILLIS Oh no. Wednesday's my half-day off. After lunch I always prepare dinner for three. Usually a simple cold meal like this one.

SILVER And where did you go?

(Dr Brown and Inspector Thackeray enter.)

MRS WILLIS Oh... Inspector! I didn't hear you both come down

THACKERAY Go ahead, Mrs Willis. I'd be glad to hear the answer myself. Where did you go?

MRS WILLIS I went to my sister's.

DR BROWN Is that the one with the little shop, in Middleton?

MRS WILLIS Yes, Doctor. I caught the three o'clock bus. I went to Mary's and stayed the night.

SILVER So you didn't get back till this morning?

MRS WILLIS That's right.

SILVER Mr Granger had dinner with either his niece or his nephew last night, sir.

THACKERAY Well, we'd better see them, hadn't we?

SILVER Where can we find them, Mrs Willis?

MRS WILLIS Well, Miss Edwards works at the airport. At least she's an air hostess. Perhaps she's the one who stayed away. She couldn't come last week either. She flies all over the world, you know. Such a nice girl. She's going to be so unhappy when she hears about this.

DR BROWN And John Edwards works at Harper's Bank, in the High Street.

SILVER Thank you sir.

THACKERAY Mrs Willis – don't throw away the food from any of these plates, will you?

MRS WILLIS Why's that, sir?

THACKERAY I have my reasons.

DR BROWN Perhaps someone put the medicine into Mr Granger's food. That's what you're thinking, Inspector, isn't it?

THACKERAY That's right.

MRS WILLIS Oh what a terrible thing to say.

DR BROWN Forget it.

SILVER Why, Doctor?

DR BROWN That medicine may look like water. But it tastes terrible.

THACKERAY You'd notice it in food?

DR BROWN Notice it? You'd have to wash your mouth out.

THACKERAY Oh well. That's the end of another idea. Right. Next, a visit to Mr John Edwards, I think. We're more likely to find him than Miss Edwards.

MRS WILLIS Oh dear. I haven't had time to phone him about poor Mr Granger. I think I'll do that now.

THACKERAY Mrs Willis!

MRS WILLIS Yes?

THACKERAY Don't phone anybody. I don't want anyone to know that he's dead. Do you understand?

MRS WILLIS Well... yes.

THACKERAY It's very important.

THURSDAY A.M:
GRANGER'S ROOM

Curtains closed

Note: room was dark when Mrs W. came in this morning

Fire

Light for reading

Book dropped on floor

G's 'usual' chair

THE CAPSULES

Hospital trying new capsule – green – less nitrine.
Earlier red capsules worked well
– Was death a medical accident? Check change of medicine.
Number of capsules – one for each day of the week, starting Monday.
By today there should still be 4 left, but only 3 in bottle.
Granger would never take 2 capsules together (Dr B sure about this).
Time of death between 9 and 10 pm
Murder? G would taste medicine in food or drink, so how?

> Why? Money?
> Who? Family? Housekeeper? Doctor? Check all movements
> for Wednesday.

MRS WILLIS

– liked house a lot (from silver)   – knew about medicine cupboard
– used to be a nurse   – made dinner before leaving
– usually gave G his medicine   for Middleton (check this)

What <u>happened</u> between 9 pm and 11 pm?

MRS WILLIS Very well.

THACKERAY Some of my men will be here in a few minutes.
They'll take the body away. Meanwhile, Sergeant
Silver and I have business at Harper's Bank. With
Mr John Edwards.

Scene 5

(Harper's Bank. John Edwards' office.)

JOHN I'm sorry I kept you waiting, gentlemen. The
bank's very busy this morning. I'm afraid I'll only
be able to give you five minutes. Please sit down.

THACKERAY Thank you, sir.

JOHN Now. What can I do for you gentlemen? Do you
want to open an account?

THACKERAY We're not here on business, Mr Edwards. We're
police.

JOHN Oh?

SILVER We thought you could help us with a few facts, sir.

JOHN I'm afraid we don't usually answer questions
about the bank's clients.

THACKERAY This isn't about one of your clients. It's about
your uncle, Mr Granger.

JOHN Oh?

THACKERAY When did you last see him, sir?

JOHN Last night. I had dinner with him. I say – there's
nothing wrong, is there?

SILVER Dinner, you said. What time was that, sir?

JOHN I got there about eight o'clock. And I left early at
half past nine – I thought he was rather tired.

THACKERAY You didn't quarrel at all?

JOHN Good heavens, no.

THACKERAY What were you talking about, just before you left?

JOHN Oh, just family things.

THACKERAY Would you mind telling us exactly?

JOHN Well... if you must know... we were talking about my sister's marriage.

SILVER That's Miss Ann Edwards, isn't it?

JOHN Oh. You know her.

SILVER She wasn't at dinner with you then, sir?

JOHN No. She's an air hostess. She's not always free.

THACKERAY What's this about a marriage, sir?

JOHN To Alan Price.

THACKERAY Who's he?

JOHN He works for a newspaper. He's a reporter.

SILVER Alan Price – I've seen that name before. Doesn't he write about crime for the Evening Standard?

JOHN *(Pause)* That's right. My uncle thinks he's the wrong man for Ann, I'm afraid.

THACKERAY Why's that, sir?

JOHN Well – for one thing. He owes rather a lot of money. And – well – Uncle Alec thinks she could marry someone better than a – crime reporter.

THACKERAY Your uncle has met Mr Price, then?

JOHN Yes. Ann sometimes brought him with her on Wednesday evenings. We always try to have dinner with Uncle Alec then. But it was no good. Price only talked about himself. Then he tried to borrow some money.

THACKERAY What did your uncle think about that?

JOHN Not very much. He certainly never invited him again.

THACKERAY So your uncle thinks Price is interested in his money, not his niece.

JOHN Yes. I must say I agree with him, but it's not my business, of course. And it isn't really yours either, is it?

SILVER So – Miss Edwards is rich, then, is she?

JOHN Really! Is there no end to these questions?

THACKERAY Try to help us sir. You have my word. It is important.

JOHN Very well then. She's not rich *now*, but she will be when my uncle dies. He'll be leaving her plenty of money.

SILVER How d'you know that, sir?

JOHN I deal with all his papers. They're at the bank here. Do you think I'm telling lies or something?

THACKERAY No, certainly not. But we do have to check. Tell us – who else would get money?

JOHN Well, *I* would. His money will be shared between Ann and myself. Except for five thousand pounds – that goes to his doctor.

THACKERAY Dr Brown, eh?

JOHN Oh, and the house and everything in it – that goes to Mrs Willis, the housekeeper.

THACKERAY One day, she'll be rich then?

JOHN One day.

THACKERAY So. We're talking about many thousands of pounds.

JOHN Oh yes. My uncle was rich. Very rich.

THACKERAY How much do *you* expect to get, for example?

JOHN Well, that depends. He had a lot of money in different companies. I'd guess… nearly half a million pounds.

THACKERAY Hmm. That *is* a lot.

JOHN But what is all this about? Why all these questions?

THACKERAY Just tell me this, Mr Edwards. Who gave your uncle his medicine last night?

JOHN His medicine? You mean those green things he gets from Dr Brown?

THACKERAY That's right. The capsules.

JOHN The capsules? He had to take one every evening – or something like that – didn't he?

THACKERAY That's right.

JOHN I don't really know. He went up to the bathroom after coffee.

THACKERAY What time was that?

JOHN After coffee. Oh about nine o'clock.

SILVER Are you saying he took the capsule himself?

JOHN Yes. Yes, I remember now. He did say he was going for his medicine then.

SILVER But you didn't *see* him take it.

JOHN No, I didn't. There *is* something wrong, isn't there?

THACKERAY Yes, I'm afraid there is. *(Pause)* Mr Edwards, I want you to prepare yourself for a big shock. *(Pause)* Your uncle is dead.

JOHN   Dead? Oh no! Poor Uncle Alec. Why didn't you tell me at the beginning? And what are all these questions about? You don't think he was killed, do you? How did it happen?

SILVER   That's just what we're trying to find out, Mr Edwards. How it happened. Was he all right when you left him?

JOHN   Certainly.

THACKERAY   Did he come to the door with you?

JOHN   No. I let myself out.

THACKERAY   What was your uncle doing when you left him? Think carefully, please – this could be very important.

JOHN   He was sitting in his usual chair. And he had a book in his hands. He was just starting to read it.

THACKERAY   Did you close the front door after you, sir?

JOHN   Of course I did. Really, Inspector. What a question!

THACKERAY   So no one could have come in by that door later?

JOHN   No. Not without a key.

THACKERAY   Do you have a key to the house?

JOHN   No, I don't.

THACKERAY   Who does?

JOHN   Just Uncle Alec and Mrs Willis, I think. Perhaps Ann has. I really don't know.

SILVER   Do you live alone, Mr Edwards?

JOHN   Yes.

SILVER   No one saw you arrive home, I suppose?

JOHN   No.

SILVER   In fact, no one saw you after you left Mr Granger?

Murder? Why would anyone kill Granger (G) if he was old and had heart trouble anyway?

Suicide? Why would a rich man with family (sees them every week) friends, interest in business etc kill himself?

Check — G's money. Who would get it? Was he going to change his will?

    — how he died. Ordinary heart attack? (Police doctor)

JOHN EDWARDS (G's nephew)
- arrived at G's house about 8 pm
- thinks G took medicine about 9 pm (after coffee)
  <u>Check</u> what he says about medicine with Mrs W and Dr B.
- left at 9.30 — G reading a book.
- saw <u>Alan Price</u> at gates as he left!

THE WILL — Mrs Willis gets the house, John and Ann Edwards get most of the money. (£5,000 to Dr B). Who needed money quickly? They could all have a motive.

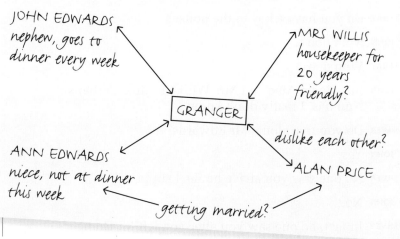

JOHN EDWARDS
nephew, goes to
dinner every week

MRS WILLIS
housekeeper for
20 years
friendly?

GRANGER

dislike each other?

ANN EDWARDS
niece, not at dinner
this week

ALAN PRICE

getting married?

JOHN No. Oh... well, yes.

SILVER Who?

JOHN Alan Price.

SILVER Where?

JOHN Outside Mr Granger's house. Near the gates. He was standing beside his car.

THACKERAY Did Mr Price see you, sir?

JOHN I think so. When I came out, he began to walk towards me. Then he turned back and got into his car. *(Pause)* You know, I really think you should stop these questions now. There'll be all kinds of things for me to do at the house. And there's all this work on my desk. You really must excuse me.

THACKERAY Yes sir. We've finished now. If you remember anything else, you'll let us know, won't you?

JOHN Yes, certainly. Where can I reach you?

THACKERAY If it's in the next hour or so, try the Evening Standard.

JOHN Oh yes. Alan Price. That's a good idea. Ask him what he was doing outside that house. I'd like to know that myself.

Scene 6

(The Evening Standard. Mr Price's office.)

ALAN PRICE Alan Price speaking... Hello? You rang me before. Well, I've just got in... Oh it's you. Well, well.

(The door of the office opens. Inspector Thackeray and Sergeant Silver enter.)

SILVER Excuse me.

ALAN Hold on, will you? Yes?

THACKERAY Mr Alan Price?

ALAN Wait outside. I'm busy just now. On the phone.

THACKERAY It's all right, sir. We'll just sit down here.

ALAN Would you mind waiting?

THACKERAY We are waiting. Have a seat, Silver. Go on, sir – finish your phone call.

ALAN Hello... I'd better ring back later... I have to get rid of a pair of jokers. They've just walked in here. What?... Yes. It lands at 13.50. An hour and a half from now. Is it important?... No!... Really? Oh well. That explains it... Yes. They're here now. Sitting in front of me... I'll ring you later. Goodbye. *(He turns to the others.)* Well, well, well

THACKERAY An interesting conversation, Mr Price.

ALAN All my conversations are interesting, Inspector. It *is* Inspector Thackeray, isn't it?

THACKERAY It is.

ALAN I remember you now. I've seen your photograph in the newspaper. You're the detective who always tries to avoid interviews, aren't you? But your friend? I don't think I've seen him before.

THACKERAY This is Sergeant Silver.

ALAN Silver...Yes, I've heard that name. You helped the Inspector on that big train robbery case, didn't you?

SILVER That's right.

ALAN Well, well, well! Let me tell you a little about myself. I write about crime, you know.

SILVER We've heard.

ALAN Oh, really? Mr Edwards told you that, did he?

THACKERAY What makes you think that?

ALAN Well, you have seen him, haven't you?

THACKERAY I didn't say that.

ALAN Oh, come on, Inspector. You don't have to keep secrets from me. We're both in the same kind of job. Crime – it makes brothers of us all.

SILVER A few questions, Mr Price, if you're ready.

ALAN Ready? I'm always ready for questions, Sergeant. And here's the first one: how did Mr Granger die?

SILVER I'm sorry? I don't understand.

ALAN Oh dear. Is he usually so slow, Inspector? Mr Granger – you know him, Sergeant. How did he die?

THACKERAY He's dead, is he?

ALAN Oh, come on now, Inspector. Of course he is.

THACKERAY How d'you know that?

ALAN Aha. That's my business.

SILVER It's also our business, Mr Price.

ALAN So – you think somebody killed him?

THACKERAY I think it's our turn to ask some questions now, Mr Price.

ALAN You may be right. I'm not doing very well with mine. All right. I'm ready.

THACKERAY What makes you think Mr Granger was killed?

ALAN Well, you wouldn't be here if he'd just died of his bad heart, would you?

SILVER That's no answer.

ALAN It's the only answer you'll get.

THACKERAY It's not good enough, though.

ALAN Well, let's just say it's my business to know these things. I'm a reporter. I write about crime, you know.

SILVER So you keep telling us.

ALAN But surely you don't think I did it?

THACKERAY Did you, Mr Price?

ALAN Oh dear, oh dear. I usually find it easy to get straight answers. You're the most difficult pair I've ever questioned.

THACKERAY Try a straight answer to this question. Where were you at half past nine last night?

ALAN Well, I think I was in my car.

THACKERAY To be exact – you were standing outside the gate of Mr Granger's house. What were you doing?

ALAN Hey – you *are* serious, aren't you?

SILVER Would you just answer the question, Mr Price?

ALAN Well, well. I was right. John Edwards has been talking. I suppose he saw me outside the gates.

THACKERAY This is the third time, Mr Price. I won't ask you again – what were you doing?

ALAN I was waiting for Ann Edwards.

SILVER There now. That was almost no pain at all, was it? Ready for another question now?

ALAN No, I think I've earned a rest, Sergeant.

THACKERAY Stop it, both of you. Mr Price – Miss Edwards doesn't live at her uncle's, does she?

ALAN No, she has her own place in town.

THACKERAY   All right – why should you wait outside her uncle's house?

ALAN   I tried to phone her. Couldn't get through. But it was a Wednesday – she usually went to her uncle's for dinner. So I went there.

THACKERAY   Why did you wait outside?

ALAN   I wasn't invited. Old man Granger didn't like me.

SILVER   You surprise me.

THACKERAY   So you expected her to come out.

ALAN   I hoped she would.

THACKERAY   Why did you want to see her?

ALAN   It's – er – rather personal.

THACKERAY   Oh, come along, Mr Price. We're all brothers in crime. We can keep a secret, you know.

ALAN   Well... we had an argument – about a week ago. I haven't seen her since.

SILVER   What was the argument about?

ALAN   Do I have to tell him?

THACKERAY   Tell me, lad. I'll understand.

ALAN   Well. It was stupid really. She'd been trying to phone me, and I was always busy. So in the end she came here – to the office.

SILVER   And?

ALAN   Well. You know how it is. You've seen my secretary?

THACKERAY   The young lady in the outside office?

ALAN   Yes. Well. She was here with me. If you've seen her, you'll know.

THACKERAY She's rather pretty, isn't she?

SILVER If you like that kind of thing.

ALAN Well – we were laughing. A few jokes. You know what I mean. Just a bit of fun. Ann didn't seem to understand. She got the wrong idea, I think.

THACKERAY Was she jealous?

ALAN Jealous? She was really angry. And then I had to make her wait until I finished writing my story. That made her worse, of course. When I took her out to dinner an hour later, she never said a word. It was all a complete waste of time. You know what women are like.

THACKERAY So after a week, you decided to end the quarrel.

SILVER By giving her a nice surprise outside her uncle's house.

ALAN The police are really quite human these days, aren't they?

THACKERAY Mr Price – just the facts, please. Miss Edwards didn't come out?

ALAN No. John Edwards came out instead.

THACKERAY Did you speak to him?

ALAN I was going to ask him if Ann was in the house. Then I changed my mind.

SILVER Why?

ALAN I decided to have a look myself.

THACKERAY You went into the house?

ALAN No. I got back in the car, and drove down the path, and then right round the house. Twice.

THACKERAY What did you expect to see?

ALAN   Her car. It wasn't there though, and the place was all dark.

THACKERAY   You're certain about that?

ALAN   Oh yes. I told you – I drove round it twice. There wasn't a light on anywhere. Don't you believe me?

SILVER   Believe you! Huh. I've read too many of your stories.

THACKERAY   This photograph on your desk. Is this young lady Miss Edwards?

ALAN   Yes. Hey – why am I telling you all this about Ann and me? I thought this was about Granger?

THACKERAY   Did you like Mr Granger?

ALAN   Me? No. Not much.

SILVER   Why not?

ALAN   He loved two things in his life. First, himself. Second, his money.

THACKERAY   Wasn't he kind to Miss Edwards?

ALAN   Kind? He invited her to dinner once a week. Gave her a present on her birthday. But he wouldn't...

THACKERAY   Yes? Go on, Mr Price. He wouldn't what?

ALAN   He wouldn't help us to get married.

SILVER   Help you? How?

ALAN   With money, of course. So we thought it would be better to wait.

THACKERAY   Until he died?

ALAN   Yes. Ann liked the old man, you know. She didn't want to hurt him. I didn't want to hurt him either, of course. It seemed stupid to hurt him and lose all that money.

THACKERAY Which money?

ALAN Oh, Inspector, please! You know. He was leaving half of his money to Ann.

THACKERAY If she didn't marry you?

ALAN Yes. Something like that.

THACKERAY So now you'll be very rich.

ALAN Yes. When we get married.

SILVER And when will that be?

ALAN I don't know. As soon as possible, I suppose.

THACKERAY And now I must ask you again. How did you know Mr Granger was dead?

ALAN Inspector Thackeray. I'm a reporter. I report a lot of stories. And do you know why? Because people tell me things. They trust me. They know I'll keep their names secret. I pay them and I forget them.

THACKERAY When we came in, you were on the phone. That wasn't a newspaper story. Somebody was telling you about me. Who was it?

ALAN Inspector – I can't tell you that. I've got my good name – my reputation – to think about.

SILVER There are tears in my eyes.

THACKERAY Who are you protecting, Mr Price?

ALAN For the last time, Inspector –

THACKERAY Would it be Miss Edwards?

ALAN How d'you mean?

THACKERAY You're clearly protecting someone. Was that Miss Edwards who phoned you just now?

ALAN Why d'you think that?

THACKERAY Did she know her uncle was dead? How did she know?

ALAN Ann loved her uncle.

SILVER But you didn't, did you?

ALAN Certainly not. I've never said I did.

THACKERAY And you were outside his house last night. Do you have a key?

ALAN No.

THACKERAY But perhaps Miss Edwards has.

SILVER Did you use her key, Mr Price?

ALAN Oh, come on, now!

SILVER Did you steal it from her? Or did she give it to you?

ALAN This is nonsense. N-o-n-s-e-n-s-e. Nonsense. Write that down in your notebook, Sergeant.

THACKERAY You said she was jealous. Perhaps she thought she was losing you. Perhaps she decided to marry you as quickly as possible.

ALAN Perhaps, perhaps, perhaps!

SILVER But to marry you, she needed money. And there was one easy way to get money. Lots of it. For a few minutes' work.

ALAN You're not saying Ann did it, are you?

SILVER Did she? While you kept guard outside?

ALAN Now that is the end. That is too much.

THACKERAY Was it you then, Mr Price? All alone?

SILVER Did you go into the house after John Edwards left?

ALAN I've told you. I drove away.

THACKERAY Yes. You've told us. But did anyone see you?

ALAN There was no one else there.

SILVER Exactly.

THACKERAY What time did you get home, Mr Price?

ALAN I didn't go straight home. I came back here to the office.

THACKERAY When did you get here?

ALAN About ten o'clock.

THACKERAY Ten o'clock? Granger's house is only a quarter of an hour from here.

SILVER And you took half an hour?

ALAN Well, perhaps it was sooner. I don't look at my watch all the time.

THACKERAY You're not very sure about last night, are you?

ALAN Perhaps not. But I was never inside that house.

SILVER Well, somebody was. And if Miss Edwards has a key she can walk in any time she wants. And somebody has just rung you – and told you Alec Granger is dead.

ALAN Well it couldn't be Ann.

THACKERAY Why not?

ALAN She's in Rome.

THACKERAY Ah. So much trouble for one little fact.

ALAN So she couldn't have rung me just now.

SILVER That's not quite true, either. They do have telephones in Rome, you know.

ALAN Oh, he's not going to start all over again, is he? Look, I'm telling the truth. That phone call was not from Ann. Now will you just forget all about her? And will you both leave my office? I have nothing else to say. And I have a lot of work to do.

ALAN PRICE

Background – Silver to check these details
– last job
– bank account
– record (no trouble with police)
– work as reporter (knows a lot about his subject – crime and
  criminals!)

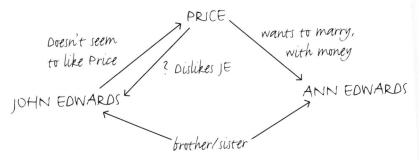

PRICE

Doesn't seem
to like Price

? Dislikes JE

wants to marry,
with money

JOHN EDWARDS

ANN EDWARDS

brother/sister

Price's phone call

Price said – "They're here now." (Who? Us?)
           – "It lands at 13.50." (Rome flight?)
           – "I'll ring you later." (Who?)

Acted v. strangely!
– knew G was dead – how?
– said, "You think somebody killed him?" WHY?
– didn't want to tell us name of caller

THACKERAY One last thing, please. You spoke about a time,
on the phone – 13.50 hours.

SILVER That's right, sir. He did. He said, "It lands at
13.50." He must have meant a plane. A plane
from Rome, perhaps?

ALAN I told you. I have nothing more to say.

THACKERAY Very well, Mr Price. We'll leave you. I think we'll take a little drive to the airport now.

SILVER And we'll see what Miss Edwards has to say.

THACKERAY Good morning, Mr Price. Don't work too hard on crime, will you. It can be dangerous.

Scene 7

(The airport waiting room. Inspector Thackeray and Sergeant Silver are sitting at a table. A plane is just landing.)

SILVER D'you know where to expect Miss Edwards?

THACKERAY Yes. She comes through this gate here. And she shouldn't be very long now. Her plane landed ten minutes ago.

SILVER D'you really think she can help us? Rome's a long way away.

THACKERAY We'll just have to wait and find out. Just think about those times, Silver. Granger died between nine and ten o'clock last night. That's what the doctor said. Where was everybody then? That's the first thing.

SILVER John Edwards was at Granger's house for half that time.

THACKERAY Yes. And Mrs Willis was at her sister's in Middleton. But it's only half an hour's bus ride back to Granger's house.

SILVER Price was outside the house for quite a long time. And that just leaves Ann Edwards.

THACKERAY Does it? What about Dr Brown? Where was he?

SILVER Oh. Here's Miss Edwards now. Coming through the gate.

THACKERAY Miss Ann Edwards?

ANN Yes?

THACKERAY Good afternoon, miss. I'm Inspector Thackeray, Manchester police. This is Sergeant Silver. We'd like to ask you a few questions.

ANN Oh. Well... all right. Will it take long?

THACKERAY Oh no. About ten minutes perhaps. Would you like something to drink?

ANN Well – yes, please. A coffee.

SILVER Milk and sugar?

ANN Yes, please.

SILVER I'll get it.

ANN Thank you, Sergeant. That's most kind of you.

(Sergeant Silver goes to the coffee bar.)

ANN What's it all about, Inspector?

THACKERAY We're hoping you can help us. You've just arrived from Rome?

ANN Yes. I've just come off the plane.

THACKERAY When were you last here in Manchester?

ANN Last night.

THACKERAY Really?

ANN Yes. My plane left at half past ten last night.

THACKERAY And when did you get to the airport here?

ANN About twenty minutes before that. Between five and ten past ten.

THACKERAY Only twenty minutes? That's a bit late, isn't it?

ANN   Yes, it is. I wasn't supposed to go at all. But one of the other hostesses fell ill. And the airport telephoned me.

THACKERAY   What time was that?

ANN   About a quarter to eight.

THACKERAY   What did you do?

ANN   Well, first I rang my brother John. We were both supposed to go to Uncle Alec's for dinner. I told him I couldn't come.

THACKERAY   So you rang him just after quarter to eight?

ANN   Yes. Just before he left.

THACKERAY   Do you have a car, Miss Edwards?

ANN   Yes.

THACKERAY   It only takes about twenty minutes from your flat to the airport here. You could have arrived at the airport at ten past eight. What happened to the other two hours?

ANN   Oh, Inspector! I had to get ready, of course. I had to wash my hair. Get some clean clothes. Press my uniform.

(Sergeant Silver comes back with the cup of coffee.)

SILVER   Here's your coffee, Miss Edwards.

ANN   Oh, thank you.

SILVER   How long since you were here in Manchester?

THACKERAY   Miss Edwards didn't leave till ten-thirty last night.

SILVER   Oh.

THACKERAY   Did you see anyone at all last night?

ANN   No. Not till I started work here. I was too busy.

THACKERAY You didn't even see Mr Price?

ANN Alan? No. Why?

THACKERAY He was seen outside your uncle's house at half past nine.

ANN Was he really?

SILVER Why do you smile, Miss Edwards?

ANN He must have thought I was there. We've had a bit of a quarrel. I haven't seen him for a week. He must have wanted to be friends again.

THACKERAY Miss Edwards, may I ask you a rather personal question?

ANN Well... That depends.

THACKERAY Are you going to marry Mr Price?

ANN I say! That *is* rather personal, isn't it?

THACKERAY Well?

ANN There's nothing the matter, is there? He's not in trouble?

SILVER Nothing that we know about, miss.

ANN Oh. Good. Well, I'd marry him now. But... it's my uncle.

THACKERAY What about him?

ANN Well, he's always been a kind of father to me. My parents died years ago. He says I'm not old enough to get married. He thinks I should wait a few years – he's not very sure about Alan. That's the real trouble.

SILVER And what are you going to do, miss?

ANN I'll try waiting. Uncle Alec may change his mind. Alan can be very nice when you really know him.

SILVER   Hmm. I'm sure, miss.

THACKERAY   Miss Edwards – do you have a key to Mr Granger's house?

ANN   Yes, I do. But why? What is all this? Has someone stolen something?

SILVER   Oh no, miss.

ANN   I'm answering all your questions. And you haven't told me anything.

LOUDSPEAKER   A message for Detective Inspector Thackeray.

SILVER   It's for you, sir.

LOUDSPEAKER   Would Detective Inspector Thackeray please come to the Enquiry Desk?

ANN   It's just over there.

LOUDSPEAKER   Detective Inspector Thackeray to the Enquiry Desk please.

THACKERAY   I won't be a minute. *(He gets up and goes to the Enquiry Desk.)*

ANN   All right, Sergeant. There's something wrong, isn't there? What is it?

SILVER   I'm afraid we have some bad news for you, Miss Edwards.

ANN   Oh no! Not Alan? You don't mean Alan?

SILVER   No, miss. It's your uncle. I'm afraid he's dead.

ANN   But... when?

SILVER   Last night, miss.

ANN   And... how?

SILVER   That's what we're trying to find out.

ANN   Oh – I should have been with him last night. Was John with him when he died?

SILVER It seems not, miss.

(The Inspector returns. He sits down again.)

THACKERAY Sorry about that. Just a phone call.

ANN Your sergeant has just told me about Uncle Alec.

THACKERAY Ah. Yes. I'm very sorry, Miss Edwards.

ANN I must go there immediately.

THACKERAY May I ask you just one more thing, miss? You've told us you rang your brother last night. Did you speak to anyone else on the phone?

ANN No. Nobody.

THACKERAY Did anyone try to telephone you?

ANN It's possible. You see, I share a flat with two other air hostesses, and the phone is often busy.

THACKERAY Was anyone with you? Did anyone see you at home?

ANN No. Why do you ask?

THACKERAY Oh, you know what policemen are like, miss. We have to check everything. But we've finished our questions now, Miss Edwards.

ANN Can I go now? I'm rather tired. *(She stands up.)*

THACKERAY Yes, of course.

(The two policemen stand up.)

SILVER We can drive you back to town if you like.

ANN I have my own car, thank you. Good afternoon.

SILVER Goodbye.

THACKERAY Good afternoon, Miss Edwards.

(Miss Edwards leaves.)

SILVER Well, sir? What was the message?

THACKERAY The police doctor's examined the body.

SILVER And?

THACKERAY It's what we thought. Dr Brown was right. Granger did take a double amount of medicine.

SILVER Two capsules. So somebody did kill him.

THACKERAY Oh yes. But I've known that for a long time.

SILVER Have you? I haven't. You don't also know who did it, do you?

THACKERAY I think so. But I'm not sure that I can prove it yet.

SILVER Why not, sir?

THACKERAY The real problem is... how? How could anyone make him take two capsules?

SILVER That's certainly a difficult one.

THACKERAY I've got to find out how it was done.

SILVER Perhaps another talk with the doctor would help.

THACKERAY Yes. Possibly. And then there are one or two loose ends to tie up.

SILVER Perhaps my notebook would help there, sir. I've written down every conversation we've had.

THACKERAY Yes. I think your notebook would help, Silver. Let's go straight back to the station. You can read it all out to me, there.

SILVER All right, sir.

THACKERAY And tomorrow morning I think I'll ask everyone to Granger's house.

SILVER What for, sir?

THACKERAY More questions. There are one or two things I'd like to check. We don't want to arrest the wrong person, do we?

Where were they between 9 and 10 pm?

1. Ann Edwards

flat ——————————→ Airport
            12 miles

Call from airport 7.45 pm   Arrived about 10.10 pm
Phoned brother straight away   Flight to Rome 10.30 pm
Left for airport 9.50

2. John Edwards'

house ——————————→ Granger's house
          5 miles   ↑

left about 7.50 pm   Alan Price was waiting at 9.30 pm
returned 9.40 pm   Saw John Edwards' car coming out at 9.30.
                  Drove round house straight after that.
                  House dark, no lights on.
                  Says he returned to office about 10.00 pm
                    – mistake? lie?

3. Alan Price
   Evening Standard office ——————↑
                   7 miles

4. Mrs Willis ——————————→ at sister's in Middleton from Wed.
        30 minutes on bus   afternoon until Thursday morning

5. Dr Brown? Check later

Ann Edwards says she was getting ready between 7.45 and 9.50 pm!!
Could she have gone to Granger's house?
– she has a car   – she has a key to the house

Scene 8

Inspector Thackeray explains

(The next morning. Inspector Thackeray, Sergeant Silver and Alan Price are waiting in the living-room of Mr Granger's house.)

ALAN How much more time before we start, Inspector? It's five past eleven already.

THACKERAY I'm afraid you'll just have to wait a little longer, Mr Price.

ALAN My newspaper won't wait though.

SILVER It'll have to.

ALAN I've got a story to write before this afternoon. *(Mrs Willis comes in.)*

MRS WILLIS I've just telephoned the bank from Mr Granger's office next door, Inspector. Mr Edwards is on his way. He won't be long.

SILVER Ah there's the bell now.

MRS WILLIS Yes, that'll be him. I'll go.

(She goes out.)

SILVER *(Shouting)* Be sure to come back in here with him, won't you Mrs Willis? We need you too.

(Mrs Willis comes back followed by Mr Edwards.)

JOHN Sorry I'm late. The bank's very busy and it's quite a long way to Uncle Alec's.

ALAN Come on, then. Sit down. Perhaps we can start now. Now then, Inspector – who killed Alec Granger?

JOHN Killed?

ALAN That's what you're going to tell us, isn't it?

MRS WILLIS Surely it was an accident?

ALAN Accidents don't interest the police.

JOHN If Uncle Alec was killed, he killed himself.

SILVER You think he committed suicide.

THACKERAY He had no reason.

JOHN He was worried about Ann marrying Mr Price here.

ALAN She'd promised she would wait for a few years.

SILVER And you don't commit suicide for something which might happen in a few years' time.

MRS WILLIS And anyway Mr Granger liked life. He'd fought hard enough to stay alive when he was in hospital last year.

THACKERAY No, Mr Edwards. Your uncle didn't kill himself. I think we can forget that.

JOHN What happened then?

THACKERAY Somebody gave him some extra medicine.

SILVER An extra capsule.

THACKERAY But your uncle didn't know that.

SILVER At first, he didn't know anything was wrong. And then suddenly, he died.

THACKERAY Now. I'm going to ask you a very important question, Mr Edwards. I want you to answer very carefully.

JOHN What's that?

THACKERAY Who knew that Mr Granger was dead on that morning?

MRS WILLIS Well, I did of course.

SILVER Ah yes. But you discovered the body.

THACKERAY So that doesn't really count.

SILVER But, Mr Price. You knew that he was dead, didn't you?

ALAN Me!

THACKERAY Surely you haven't forgotten? You made no secret of it when we came to see you yesterday.

SILVER "So – you think somebody killed him." Those were your own words. I have them here in my notebook.

JOHN Why did you say that, Mr Price?

ALAN That's my business.

THACKERAY I must warn you, Mr Price if you don't tell us, you're in serious trouble.

ALAN Nothing to say.

THACKERAY Right – Sergeant?

MRS WILLIS Oh, stop all this. It's all my fault.

JOHN You?

THACKERAY Hmm. I thought it might be.

MRS WILLIS It was because of Ann. Miss Edwards. I tried to telephone her, Inspector, after you'd left. She really loved her uncle. I thought I ought to tell her straight away.

SILVER But she wasn't at home.

MRS WILLIS No. And I didn't know when she'd be back. I just had to find out. So I rang Mr Price. He often knows where she is.

ALAN She wanted to talk to Ann quickly, Inspector. I wanted to know why.

THACKERAY So you told him that Mr Granger was dead, Mrs Willis.

MRS WILLIS Yes.

THACKERAY And you told him about me. You said the police were asking questions. And seeing Mr Edwards.

MRS WILLIS Yes. I'm sorry. I didn't mean to. I just wanted to ask about Miss Edwards really.

JOHN You can't blame her for that, Inspector.

SILVER Why couldn't you tell us all this, Mr Price?

MRS WILLIS I told him not to. The Inspector had warned me not to make any telephone calls.

ALAN And I do have my professional reputation to think about, Sergeant.

THACKERAY Your professional reputation. Mm. You were outside this house on Wednesday night, Mr Price.

ALAN That's right.

SILVER And you drove round the house in your car.

ALAN Twice.

THACKERAY What did you see?

ALAN I told you. Nothing. The place was completely dark.

THACKERAY Did you see when the lights were switched off?

ALAN No. I didn't notice exactly.

SILVER But the lights were on when you were waiting outside the gate.

ALAN Oh yes. Otherwise I wouldn't have stayed.

THACKERAY And they were off when you went to the house.

ALAN Yes.

MRS WILLIS They weren't on the next morning either. The room was quite dark when I got in.

THACKERAY Now that's very strange, Mr Edwards, isn't it?

JOHN Is it? Why?

THACKERAY Because, just as your uncle started to read, the lights went off.

JOHN Did they?

SILVER That's what you told us. You said he started to read as you were leaving.

THACKERAY But you can't read when the light's out, can you?

JOHN I suppose not.

THACKERAY And you can't go upstairs and take an extra capsule in the dark either.

SILVER So who switched the light out?

THACKERAY *(Pause)* But that's not the only strange thing about your story.

JOHN What do you mean by that?

THACKERAY You knew about Mr Granger's death long before we told you in the bank yesterday.

JOHN That's nonsense. How could I?

MRS WILLIS I didn't tell him Inspector. I only telephoned Mr Price.

ALAN And I never spoke to him all day.

JOHN You see.

SILVER Then why did you say: "My uncle was rich."

JOHN Well he was. What's wrong with that?

THACKERAY Nothing – except you said it before we told you of his death.

SILVER Was rich. Not "My uncle is rich," but "My uncle was rich."

JOHN I never said that. You've made a mistake, Sergeant.

THACKERAY No. You've made the mistake, Mr Edwards.

SILVER And you made another straight after. "He had a lot of money in different companies," you said.

THACKERAY Had, had, had, Mr Edwards. You were already talking about a dead man.

SILVER But we only mentioned his death later.

MRS WILLIS Oh, Mr Edwards!

ALAN It's only a word, Inspector. You'll need some better proof than that.

THACKERAY But that wasn't the only thing you knew, Mr Edwards. You knew about the medicine.

JOHN We all knew about that.

MRS WILLIS That's quite true, Inspector. Everybody knew about Mr Granger's capsules.

SILVER I wonder. Did you know about the capsules, Mr Price?

ALAN Of course.

SILVER Then let me ask you a simple question. What colour were they?

ALAN Colour? I've no idea.

THACKERAY Mrs Willis?

MRS WILLIS Green. They were new ones. He began taking them this week. I gave them to him on Monday and Tuesday.

SILVER Mr Edwards – you also knew the colour of the new capsules. How?

JOHN I didn't. This is the first I've heard of it.

THACKERAY Your notebook again, Sergeant.

SILVER … When asked about Mr Granger's medicine, you said, "You mean those green things from Dr Brown?"

THACKERAY Yes. Those green things, Mr Edwards. How could you know that?

MRS WILLIS Yes. How could you, Mr Edwards? You hadn't come here earlier this week.

THACKERAY And they had always been red before.

JOHN Well – I knew – because – because I gave him the capsule myself. That's right. I gave him the medicine.

THACKERAY That's not what you told us yesterday.

SILVER No sir. "Mr Granger went up to the bathroom alone," – that's what you said yesterday. According to you, he took the medicine himself. And you didn't even see it.

THACKERAY Well now, Mr Edwards. One story yesterday, and another story today. Which are we to believe?

JOHN What I'm saying now is true. Now.

SILVER Then why did you lie to us yesterday?

JOHN I… I was afraid. Yes, I was afraid.

ALAN What were you afraid of?

JOHN Them. The police.

THACKERAY But why, sir?

JOHN I thought you might accuse me.

SILVER Accuse you?

JOHN Yes.

THACKERAY Is that the real reason you were afraid?

JOHN Yes. It's true. You might think that I'd killed him.

THACKERAY But if that's true, you already knew he was dead.

JOHN I... I don't know... I'm all confused... You're making me say these things. You all heard him.

MRS WILLIS Mr Edwards – the Inspector has only asked questions. What are you saying?

ALAN He's saying he killed Alec Granger.

JOHN I didn't do it. I tell you, it's not true.

SILVER Come along, sir. It's best if you tell us now.

JOHN I didn't kill him. I didn't. How could I? Uncle Alec would never have taken two capsules. He knew that it would kill him.

THACKERAY But he didn't take two capsules. He only took one. The capsules were soft, Dr Brown said. And each one was only half full. So it was easy. Mr Edwards used the syringe.

ALAN Which syringe?

MRS WILLIS Of course. The syringe in the medicine cupboard next to the bottle of capsules.

SILVER He stuck the needle of the syringe into one capsule. He then drew the medicine out of it.

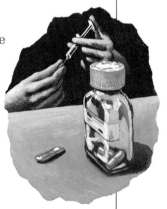

MRS WILLIS And emptied it into another capsule.

ALAN And threw the empty capsule away. Very clever.

JOHN But not clever enough.

THACKERAY John Michael Edwards, I'm arresting you for the murder of Alec Lindsay Granger. I must warn you that anything you say...

READING ACTIVITIES

Before reading

1 Each Inspector Thackeray play is a 'whodunit.' This means you do not find out who did the crime until the very end of the story.
What other 'whodunits' do you know? They might be from a book, a play or a film. Use these headings to make a list.

Writer   *Name of story*   *Crime*

Why do you think 'whodunits' are so popular?

2 Read about the first crime on the back cover of the book and look at the picture on page 3. What do you think has happened here? Write a short headline for the next day's newspaper.

While reading

1 In Scene 3 of the first play, Inspector Thackeray says the robbery is 'probably an inside job'. He must go to three different places to ask questions. Fill in his appointment diary below:

Wednesday 23 October

a.m.   p.m.

10.30 ....   2.00 ....

12.00 ....

2 As you read, or listen to each play, make your own 'detective's notes'. Look carefully at people's stories in each scene. Do they agree? There are at least three clues to lead you to the criminal in each case.

3 A detective only needs the answers to these five questions about a crime:

Who (did it)? When...? Where...? How...? Why...?

Write full questions and answers for the police record in *Dangerous medicine.*

After reading

1 "Detectives work best in pairs." Do you think this is true of Thackeray and Silver? Why?

2 Write a short description of two detectives who work together. What makes them a good team? How do they solve crimes together?